THE HISTORY OF MADRID
WRITTEN FOR CHILDREN

Pedro López Carcelén / Miguel Gómez Andrea

ediciones
LA LIBRERÍA

Acknowledgements:
Lola, Clara, Noel and Merlín;
   Nieves, Daniel, Peyo
   and the whole team at Ediciones La Librería

1ˢᵗ edition: 2017
2ⁿᵈ edition: 2018

© 2018, Miguel Gómez Andrea
© 2018, Pedro López Carcelén

© De la traducción, Justin Peterson

© 2018, Ediciones La Librería
   Calle Mayor, 80 - 28013 Madrid
   Tel. 91 541 71 70
   www.edicioneslalibreria.com

ISBN: 978-84-9873-348-8
Depósito Legal: M-1764-2017

Printed in Spain

I don't like history. It's boring and nothing ever happens. You go to sleep in the winter, you wake up in the spring, forage for fruit, catch some fish, and go wandering through the woods. It's fun when the cubs are born. They're really cute, but before you know it the autumn is over, winter comes again, and it's back to the cave. And so the years go by, one after another. We bears have always done the same thing.

I'd like to be human. Now *your* history is exciting. In fact, you might even say that the only history that really counts is yours. Look, for thousands of years there were hills and forests, lots of forests, along the banks of the Manzanares River. At first it was only us animals, and then humans arrived.

It was all very nice, but we the only thing we did was go around looking for food, to be able to sleep on a full stomach. One day humans invented agriculture and began to grow crops and raise livestock. Later they made roads and built houses, and then a castle, and then a wall, and then a town. More and more people came, and made larger and larger buildings. And, in the end, there appeared a big city where there was once only a field.

It's amazing! Now *that* is a story worth telling: how a city came to be and grew. Today Madrid is enormous, but a lot had to happen to make it what it is today. If we learn about those things we will understand each other better. I mean, *you* will understand each other better, because we bears in Madrid are history, which is why I can tell you about it.

Besides this page, I'm hiding on another 10. Can you find me?

Prehistory

BEFORE MANKIND

Before mankind there was no history, but you should know that the banks of the Manzanares River were lined with immense forests, and there were fertile and abundant lands that allowed many animals to live here for millions of years. In the place where Madrid would later arise there converged waters running down from the Sierra de Guadarrama mountains. This, as you will later see, was critical.

THE DAWN OF MAN

Almost one million years ago the first men, your ancestors, came to the Iberian Peninsula from Africa. They differed little from the other animals. At first they probably did not even hunt, but gathered fruit from the trees, dug up roots and, if they were lucky enough to find an animal, killed by lightning bolt or a fall, took advantage of their find and ate it. Over the centuries your predecessors became more human, walked more upright, crafted stone tools, honed their hunting techniques, and buried their dead with religious rites.

Your most direct ancestor, *Homo sapiens*, lived in the region of Madrid some 40,000 years ago.

Urg the Cro-Magnon (Age 3)

My father is the strongest of them all. And the best hunter. I like raw meat, but my mother always wants to burn it in the fire. It's disgusting. Raw spiders and lizards are yummy!

Mammals from the Tertiary Period (More than 1.8 million years ago)

Micromeryx   *Chalicothere*   *Listriodon*   *Anchitherium*   *Gomphothere*

Quaternary Period mammals (1 million years ago)

Aurochs   *Woolly mammoth*   *Bison*   *Irish elk*   *Human*

This image of the valley of the Manzanares River is, actually, impossible. During the Quaternary Period many of the mammals from the Tertiary had disappeared or evolved due to deglaciation. Others had not yet appeared. From which of the two periods are there more mammals in the illustration?

THE CARPETANI

Over time and through the development of agriculture and livestock, different cultures and peoples arose. In the region of Madrid some Celtic tribes settled, who had crossed the Pyrenees around 1,000 BC. They mixed with the Iberians already living here, giving rise to the Carpetani people.

The Romans called the Madrid region Carpetania because it was very flat, allowing them to use carts they called *carpentos*.

The Carpetani liked to raise horses, and built their villages and forts on top of hills. They were great warriors, and the Romans had to fight hard to defeat them.

Flavia Minimus (Age 7)

When my father left the Roman legion we opened a hostel on the road crossing Carpetania. My mother says that many people pass through the region, so we'll have lots of guests. And she's right. Every day different people come.

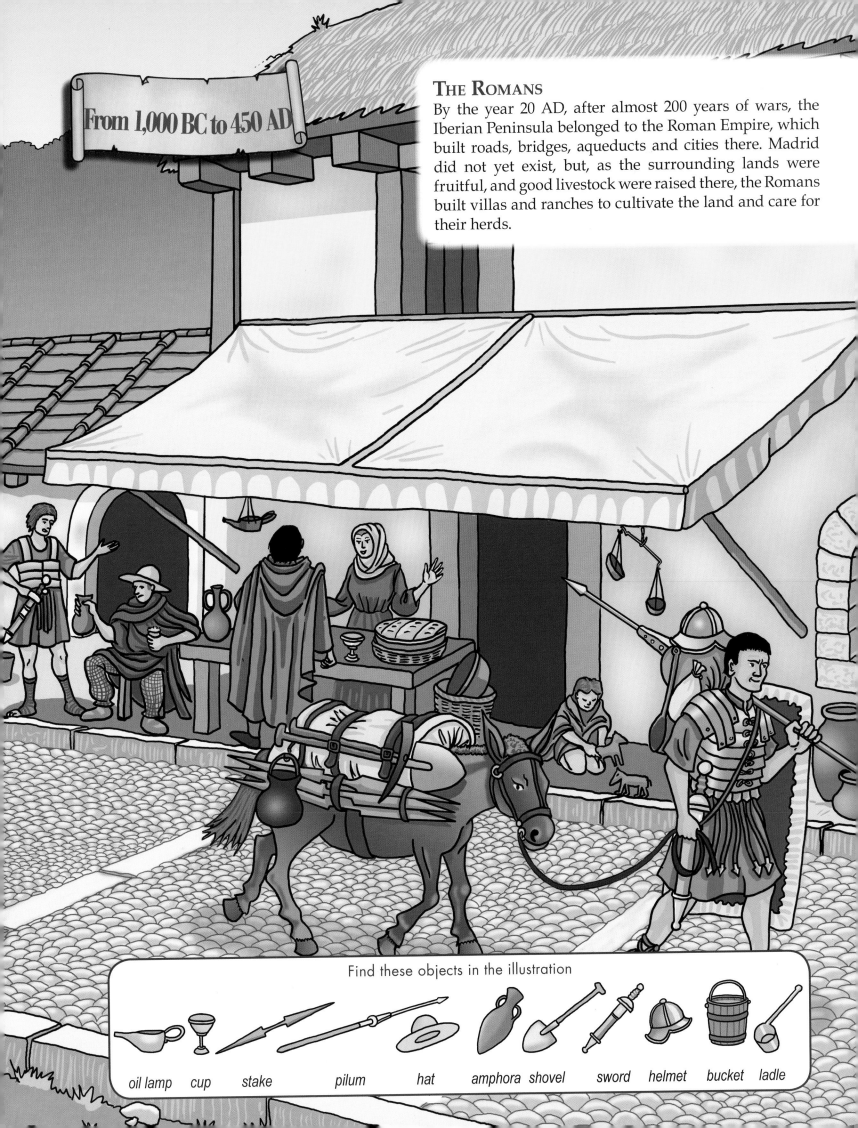

From 1,000 BC to 450 AD

THE ROMANS

By the year 20 AD, after almost 200 years of wars, the Iberian Peninsula belonged to the Roman Empire, which built roads, bridges, aqueducts and cities there. Madrid did not yet exist, but, as the surrounding lands were fruitful, and good livestock were raised there, the Romans built villas and ranches to cultivate the land and care for their herds.

Find these objects in the illustration

oil lamp   cup   stake   pilum   hat   amphora   shovel   sword   helmet   bucket   ladle

Yusuf Ibn Arabí (Age 4)
Our teacher says that the real holy war is the struggle to be better people each day. He's silly. How can I fight against myself? When I grow up I'll fight in the wars against the Christians.

THE VISIGOTHS

Everything in life comes to an end, and even the Roman Empire eventually did too. The Roman government gave way to the Visigoths, a people from Northern Europe who occupied the Iberian Peninsula. Some say that the name "Madrid" was taken from a Visigoth village. It's possible but we don't know if that is true.

THE MUSLIMS

In 711 the Muslims crossed the Strait of Gibraltar. In a very short time they defeated the Visigoths' King Roderic (Rodrigo) and seized control of the Peninsula. The Christians were pushed northward, and there began a struggle to take back the kingdom they had lost. For over 200 years the Madrid area was a borderland inhabited by both Christians and Muslims, and the site of continuous battles. It was dubbed the "Middle March."

EL ALCÁZAR

To protect the city of Toledo and an ancient Roman road, the Muslims built palace/castle/fortress complexes, which they called *alcázars*, throughout the Middle March. In the year 856, Al Mundhir, son of the emir of Cordoba, oversaw the construction of a fortress along the Manzanares River. This marked the founding of Madrid.

Bear-Dog   Listriodon   Antiquerio   Hispanotherium

Bison   Cainotherium   Aurochs   Human tool

Locate these fossils and archaeological remains that appeared during the construction of the wall.

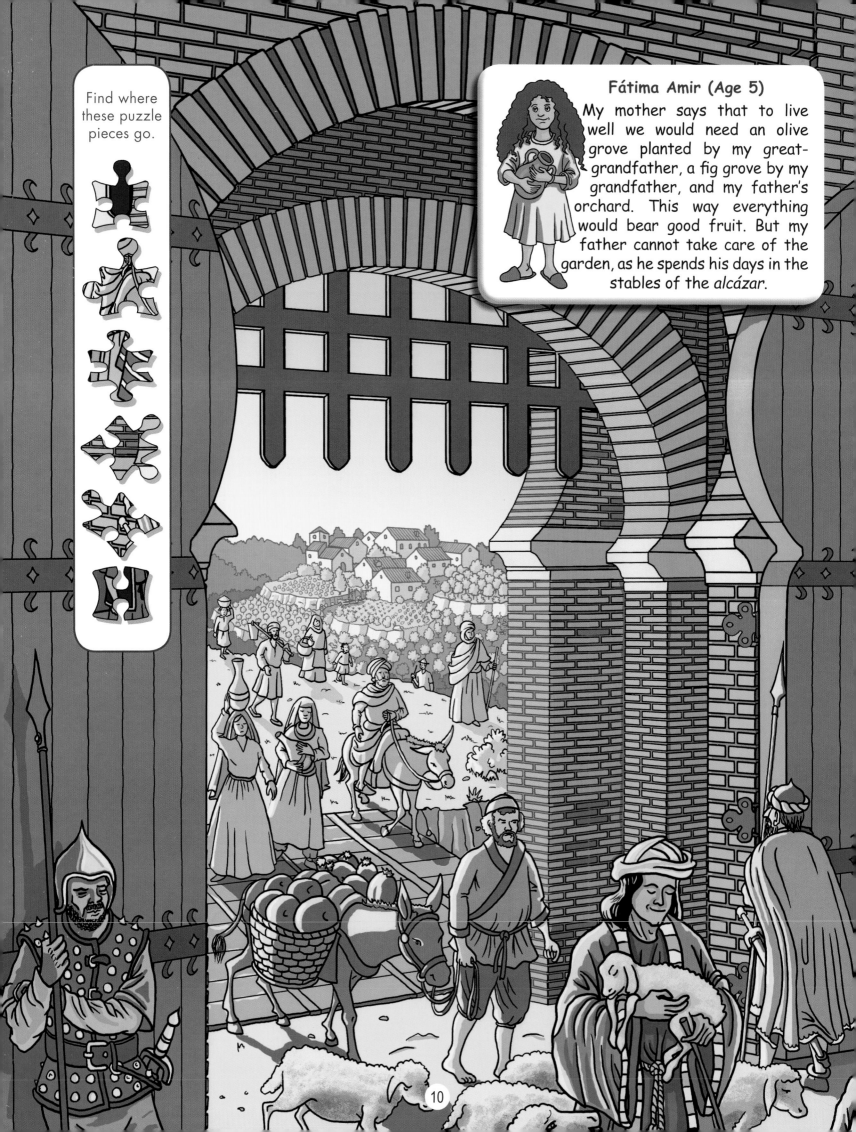

Find where these puzzle pieces go.

Fátima Amir (Age 5)
My mother says that to live well we would need an olive grove planted by my great-grandfather, a fig grove by my grandfather, and my father's orchard. This way everything would bear good fruit. But my father cannot take care of the garden, as he spends his days in the stables of the *alcázar*.

From 856 to 950

MAYRIT

Around the *alcázar* there emerged a small village that the Muslims called Mayrit, a word meaning "mother of the waters." They called it this due to the abundance of springs and streams there. The word evolved over time. The Christians transformed "Mayrit" into "Magerit," and centuries later "Magerit" became "Madrid."

LOS VIAJES DE AGUA (WATER CHANNELS)

The Muslims, expert farmers and masters of irrigation techniques, invented *viajes de agua*, a system of tunnels running from underground springs to bring water to people. Madrid's streets and orchards were irrigated by them.

THE WALL AND SAN ANDRÉS QUARTER.

In the shadow of the *alcázar* (palace/castle/fortress), Mayrit gradually grew. A mosque was built, and a wall protected its people from the dangers of war. There were many Christians who refused to convert to the Muslims' religion, but they learned their language and customs. These Christians were called *mozárabes*, or Mozarabs, and they were not allowed to live inside the walls. The Mozarabs built the church of San Andrés (St. Andrew) and, around it, their quarter.

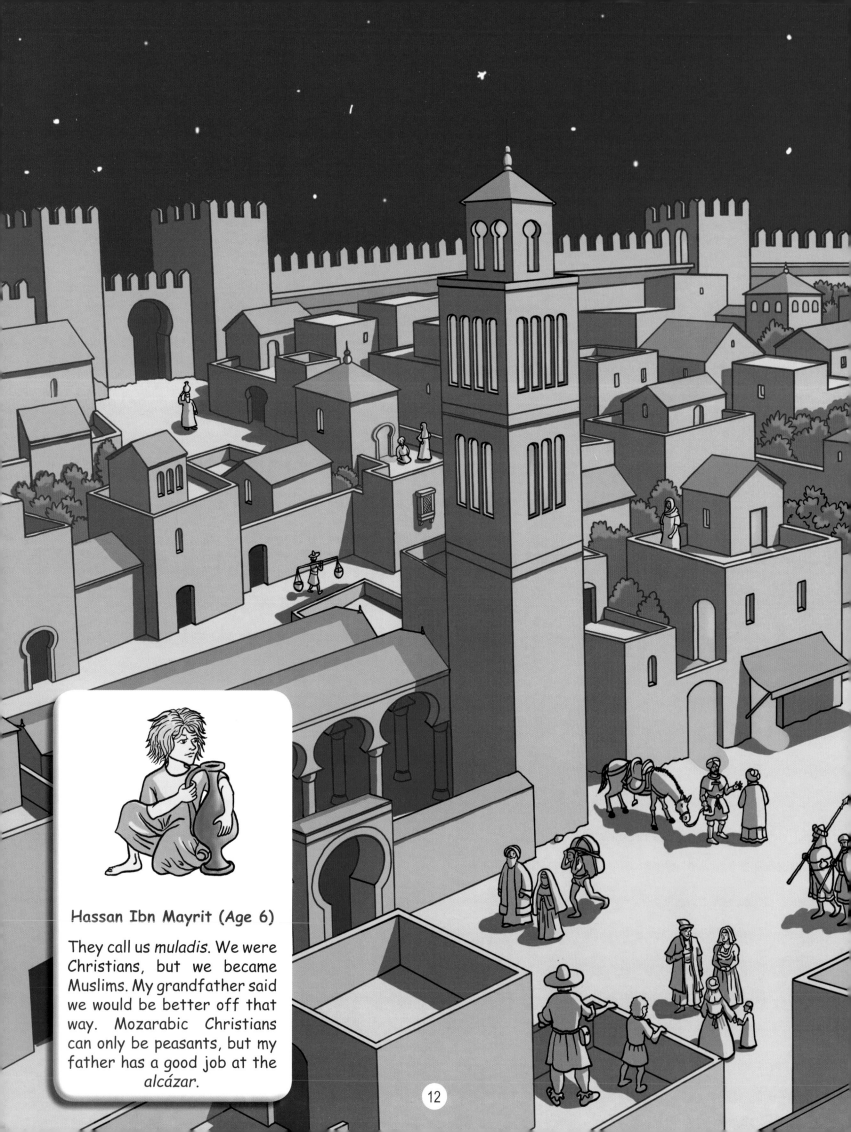

Hassan Ibn Mayrit (Age 6)

They call us *muladis*. We were Christians, but we became Muslims. My grandfather said we would be better off that way. Mozarabic Christians can only be peasants, but my father has a good job at the *alcázar*.

From 951 to 1080

MAYRIT'S PROSPERITY

A Muslim scholar once said that there are five things a city needs to flourish: running water, fertile land, a nearby forest for wood, strong walls, and a leader who keeps the peace. All these conditions existed in Mayrit, which, although not quite a city, was a town of some importance. On the streets of its medina one could find Mozarabic Christians, Berber Muslims from North Africa, Arabs, Jews and *Muladis*.

They say that in Mayrit there were up to seven schools of Astronomy, at which the stars were studied. The *alcázar* was so large that the Muslim leader of Córdoba, Almanzor, gathered his troops here before crossing the Sierra de Guadarrama mountain range to wage war against the Christians.

CHRISTIAN ATTACKS

But the Christians continued with their *Reconquista*. There were many battles, and knights attacked Mayrit more than once. Ramiro III of León lay siege to Mayrit, and knocked down its walls, but had to withdraw when reinforcements arrived for its defence. One hundred years later, Ferdinand I, King of Castile, besieged Mayrit again, but was unable to conquer it either.

| Jew | Berber | Slave | Arab | Mozarab | Muladi |

Locate these Madrilenians of different races and religions.

THE CHRISTIAN CONQUEST

In 1083 Alfonso VI the Brave, King of Castile and León, took the city of Toledo and, with it, Mayrit, wresting them from the Muslims. At this point many things changed in the old Muslim town. The Mozarabic Christians left their area of San Andrés and moved within the walls. The mosque was converted into the Church of Santa María, and the Muslims had to move to the outskirts. The Christian kings proclaimed that Madrid was to be considered a major town, or *villa*, which meant that its people had their own laws, and lands held in common.

Beltrán Salvado (Age 8)

I had fallen into a well and I was going to drown. Isidore got the waters to rise and lift me out. A miracle. When Isidore prays, the angels plough the field for him, and his lord, Mr Vargas, does not get angry with him.

St. Isidore The Labourer

At that time there was born in Magerit a humble farmer who also worked as a well-digger. He was a good, devout man who prayed to the Virgin every day, and always aided those in need by sharing his food with them. His wife was named María de la Cabeza and was also very pious. Isidore lived to a ripe age and when he died, his fame was so great that many considered him a saint, and ended up naming him the town's patron saint.

In this illustration there are seven little animals that you will able to find on pages 28-29, 44-45 and 60-61. Find them and you'll able to see, along the way, how Madrid has changed over the years.

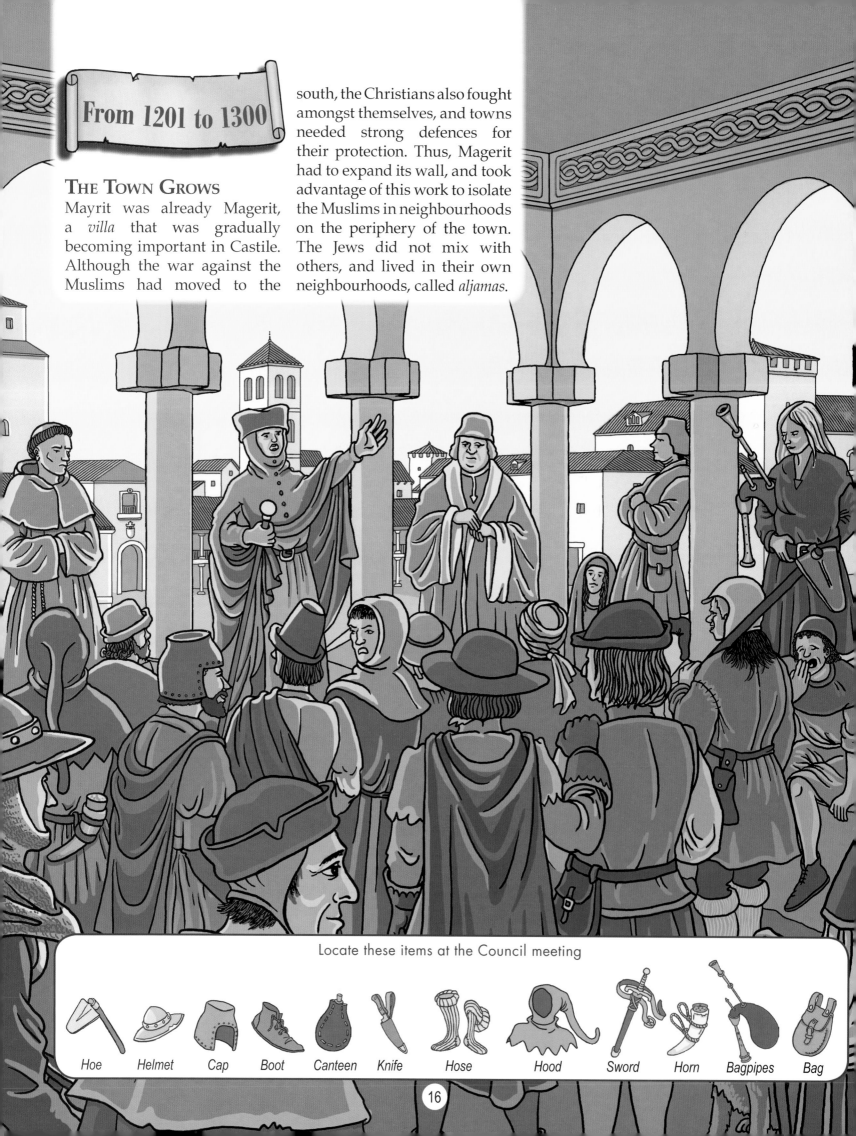

THE TOWN GROWS

Mayrit was already Magerit, a *villa* that was gradually becoming important in Castile. Although the war against the Muslims had moved to the south, the Christians also fought amongst themselves, and towns needed strong defences for their protection. Thus, Magerit had to expand its wall, and took advantage of this work to isolate the Muslims in neighbourhoods on the periphery of the town. The Jews did not mix with others, and lived in their own neighbourhoods, called *aljamas*.

Locate these items at the Council meeting

Hoe Helmet Cap Boot Canteen Knife Hose Hood Sword Horn Bagpipes Bag

EL CONCEJO ABIERTO (THE OPEN COUNCIL)

In those days the kings did not wield much power, and the roads were in bad condition, and dangerous. In winter it was difficult to travel from one place to another, which meant that towns and cities were largely independent, and governed by their own laws, called *fueros*. In Madrid, when it was necessary to resolve an issue affecting the people, they rang the bells of the Church of San Salvador and all the people gathered in an Open Council. There anyone could speak, and decisions were eventually made by votes cast by the men.

Mario Avendaño (Age 9)

We Jews are not allowed to cultivate the land or be soldiers. As some of us work collecting the king's taxes, the Christians resent us. My father is a doctor and cures people, so people like him.

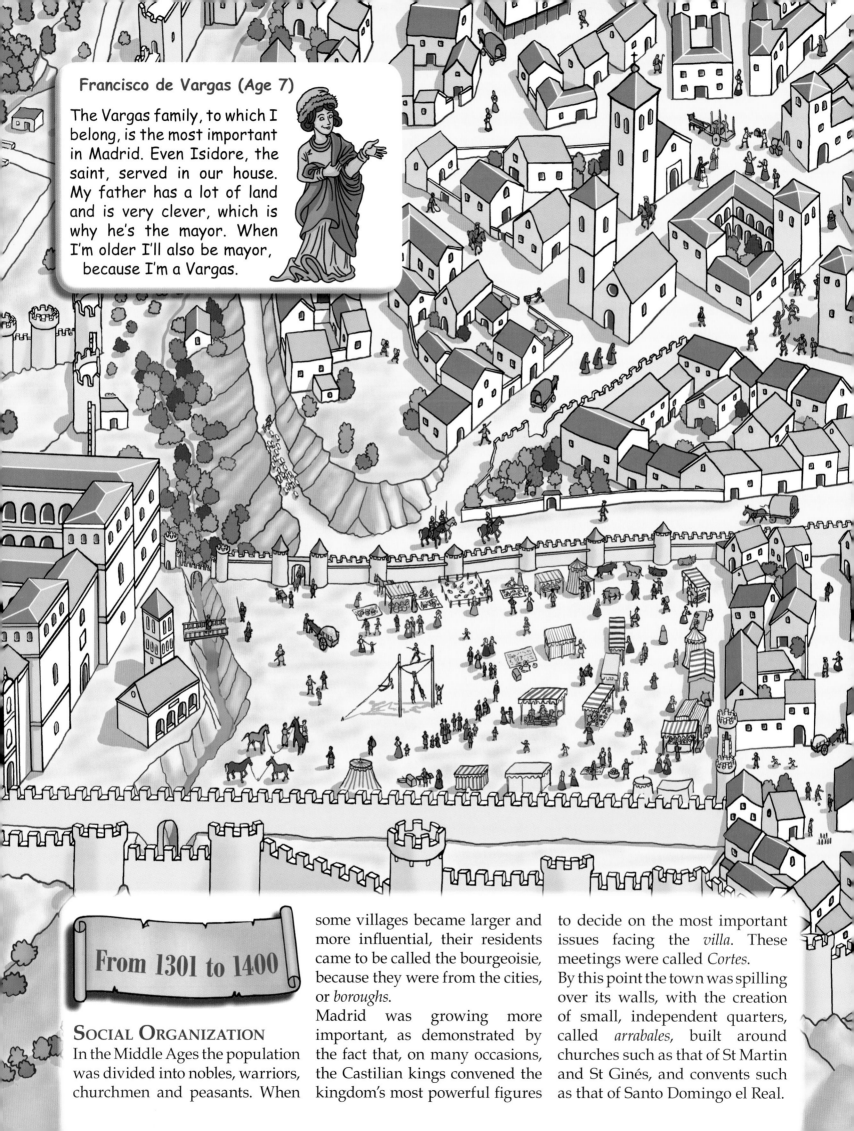

Francisco de Vargas (Age 7)

The Vargas family, to which I belong, is the most important in Madrid. Even Isidore, the saint, served in our house. My father has a lot of land and is very clever, which is why he's the mayor. When I'm older I'll also be mayor, because I'm a Vargas.

From 1301 to 1400

SOCIAL ORGANIZATION

In the Middle Ages the population was divided into nobles, warriors, churchmen and peasants. When some villages became larger and more influential, their residents came to be called the bourgeoisie, because they were from the cities, or *boroughs*.

Madrid was growing more important, as demonstrated by the fact that, on many occasions, the Castilian kings convened the kingdom's most powerful figures to decide on the most important issues facing the *villa*. These meetings were called *Cortes*.

By this point the town was spilling over its walls, with the creation of small, independent quarters, called *arrabales*, built around churches such as that of St Martin and St Ginés, and convents such as that of Santo Domingo el Real.

Around the year 1346 King Alfonso XI decided that there would be no more open councils, and that *villas* were to have mayors, councillors and other officers. Thus was born the city council. The people no longer decided freely, and local affairs were handled by a group of people chosen from amongst the important families.

Locate these scenes in the illustration.

The Middle Ages

Benjamín Travieso
(Age 5)

The priest tells us to pray for the plague to go away. I believe that God is angry, so he is punishing us and making us go hungry. But I don't care, because I always find something to eat.

Find the 18 rats and mice in the illustration.

HUNGER

In those days people ate what the fields gave them, and meat was reserved for holidays. The most important food was wheat bread. During good years, when the harvests were abundant, the leftover wheat was kept in large silos. Many years it did not rain enough, or too much, and the crops were ruined. If this happened several years in a row, the wheat reserves ran out, and the people, with nothing to eat, began to starve.

THE PLAGUE

In the Middle Ages Madrid was a very dirty city. Waste was thrown into the street, and homes had no bathrooms. Many pigs, chickens and animals were left loose, wandering wherever they wanted. There then appeared a very serious and contagious disease, the plague, which killed many people. As there was no hygiene, the disease was quickly spread by rats and insects. When the plague hit, the cities and fields were filled with dead bodies.

The Middle Ages

MADRID KEEPS GROWING

During this period Madrid grew steadily to the east of the Manzanares River. On the other side, in what is today the Casa de Campo green area, there stood only the Vargas family palace. A large portion of the old walls, with their 190 towers, were obscured and enclosed by the new city's narrow, winding streets. The first markets were held in the Plaza de la Paja and the Campo del Rey.

MEDIEVAL WARS

During the struggles for power in medieval Castile, the *alcázar* of Madrid was attacked many times, as the people of the city fought back from within its walls.

Our *villa*, however, always fought on the losing side: it supported King Peter I, who was defeated by his stepbrother Henry II, and 100 hundred years later it backed Princess Joanna in her failed war against the future Queen Isabella the Catholic. In the end, as in all wars, those who suffered most were the people that had nothing to do with the affairs of the powerful.

Felisa Expósito (Age 10)

My brothers died of starvation. The plague took my mother, and my father was killed at the *alcázar*. Now the nuns take care of me. I clean and bring them firewood, so they let me eat and sleep at the convent.

Lance

Sword

Shield

Dagger

Mace

Bascinet

Crossbow

Chain mal cap

Axe

Pike

Locate these weapons on the medieval warriors.

From 1350 to 1474

FESTIVALS AND TOURNAMENTS

The kings of Castile were always traveling from one castle to another to oversee what was happening in their kingdom. They liked to come to Madrid to enjoy its forests, waters and clean air. Many nobles and servants travelled with them. When they arrived the city took on a livelier air. King Henry IV spent long periods at the *alcázar* and organised tournaments, great hunts, and parties to enjoy himself in the company of his knights and ladies.

THE MARKET

To help the city King Henry IV granted Madrid permission to hold a large market at which to buy and sell all kinds of things: from a lamb to a donkey, from shoes to pots and pans. The markets back then were held inside the walls, in the Plazuela de San Salvador, today the Plaza de la Villa. Artisans, merchants and farmers from other towns and cities came to sell their products. The markets made Madrid more important and, as genuine fairs, made it a festive place for as long as they lasted.

Pascuala Arcilla (Age 7)

At the last market we sold everything. Madrid's potters are famous throughout Castile. They say that the mud with which we make our pots is the best. But it's not only the mud. We're also the best potters.

Find these characters in the crowd at the market held in the Plazuela de San Salvador.

Soldier   *Morisca*   *Friar*   *Minstrel*   *Lady*   *Gentleman*   *Jew*   *Baker*

From 1475 to 1500

THE CATHOLIC KINGS

After winning the war for the crown, the new kings, Ferdinand and Isabella, began to rule with a stronger hand. In Madrid they issued new laws calling for the streets to be clean and lit. They fixed the wall and enclosed the different neighbourhoods, securing the city's gates. They did so because those who wished to sell animals or goods in the *villa* had to pay a fee at the gate before entering, called a *portazgo*. The Catholic Monarchs spent long periods in Madrid, not only to issue laws, but also to hunt in the woods of El Pardo, where one could still find bears. Ferdinand and Isabella were called the Catholic Kings called because they decided that their religion should be the only one in Spain, so they banished all the Jews and Muslims who refused to convert to Christianity.

Jacinto Montero (Age 10)

The kings have always liked to hunt in Madrid's forests, and I help my father with the dogs. They hurt or kill the boars and bears, of which I am very fond, so that makes me sad.

Apart from the horses, dogs and bears, in the illustration there are 20 more little animals. Find them.

EMPEROR CHARLES

The Catholic Monarchs were succeeded by their grandson Charles V, in turn, a grandson of the Austrian Emperor Maximilian. To maintain his European empire Charles V had to spend his life waging war, and only came to Spain to raise money to pay for the country's armies. This was one of the causes of the War of the Communities, in which Madrid, as always, came out on the losing side. Victorious, the emperor gave Madrid as a residence to his son, the future Philip II. The old *alcázar* was then reformed, converted into the Palace of the Habsburgs. Charles V, weary of so many wars, abandoned the Spanish throne in 1556. The new king, Philip II hired architect Juan de Herrera, who designed the Bridge of Segovia, to draw up plans for the construction of the massive Monastery of San Lorenzo de El Escorial. And he also made the most fateful decision in Madrid's history.

Dorita Jabones (Age 5)

My mother is a washerwoman down by the river, and I come with her every day. She leaves the sheets very white, and is very happy because the Manzanares doesn't have much water, so if she falls in she doesn't drown.

In this illustration there are seven little animals that you will able to find on pages 14-15, 44-45 and 60-61. Find them and you'll able to see, along the way, how Madrid has changed over the years.

Evaristo Tintero (Age 9)
In Valladolid my father worked as a clerk for the Council of Castile. Now we've had to come to Madrid, and for months we've been sleeping in the stables of the *alcázar* because we can´t find anywhere else to live. I'm learning to write, so I don't end up cleaning stables.

30

MADRID AS THE CAPITAL

As you know, the Castilian kings always travelled with their entourage from one city to another. In the year 1561 Philip II decided to establish the capital of his kingdom in Madrid. All the officials in charge of administrating the realm had to come and live in the city, and the nobles, who always followed the king, had to build palaces for themselves. In short, the city filled with people who had nowhere to live. To solve this problem the king enacted a law stating that all those who had large houses were obliged to sell or rent part of them to accommodate the officials.

From 1562 to 1600

LAS CASAS A LA MALICIA (HOUSES OF MALICE)

The people did not like this new law at all, so they began building houses which, seen from the street, seemed to be small and to have only one level, unable to accommodate anyone else. But this was all a trick, as in reality they had second floors and plenty of space. These houses, built to get around the law, were called *Casas a la Malicia*.

Locate these objects

Brush   Hammer   Pliers   Barrel   Weather vane   Bonnet   Stewpot   Boot

31

Find these characters in the Plaza Mayor.

Gentleman   Lady   Blind minstrel   Clergyman

Lady merchant   Soldier   Mule driver   Porter

From 1601 to 1620

THE MADRID KING

Madrid had some 60,000 inhabitants when Philip II died and was succeeded by Philip III, the first king born in Madrid. One of the new king's first decisions was to move the capital from Madrid to Valladolid. You can imagine how the people of Madrid reacted to that. After having to beg him, and even pay him, five years later Philip III decided to move the court back to the city where he was born. At that time Madrid was not only the capital of Spain, but also of the Spanish Empire, which extended throughout America and half of Europe. It was a city full of churches and convents of the many religious orders.

LA PLAZA MAYOR (THE MAIN SQUARE)

The king hired architect Juan Gómez de Mora to build a square worthy of the capital of the world's largest empire. In just a few years the Plaza Mayor was constructed, which became the centre of life in Madrid. In it there were markets, civil and religious trials, bullfights, and all kinds of festivities. If you want to know what Philip III looked like, you can view the statue standing today in the centre of the Plaza Mayor.

Seforita Manzanas (Age 8)

How lovely our Plaza Mayor is! My mother says it's like magic, in just two years having a square with so many buildings and floors. A lot of people fit in it, and the market is very good for selling our fruit.

33

Marujita Aspavientos (Age 7)

I'm going to be an actress like my mother, María La Calderona, who is so good that even the king disguises himself to come and see her. But we all know it's him by the giddy face he makes whenever my mother comes out.

Find these hats in the Corral de Comedias.

Cap   Wide-brimmed   Birreta   Straw hat   Feathered hat   Top hat   Bonnet   Helmet

From 1550 to 1650

THE GOLDEN AGE
The last 100 years have been called the Golden Age in Spanish history because during them, in addition to being one of the most powerful countries in the world, Spanish culture produced a number of great painters and writers. Authors like Quevedo, Góngora and Lope de Vega could run into Cervantes on the streets of the city's "District of Letters," where they all lived.

Painters like Diego Velázquez, Ribera and Murillo, were also illustrious residents of Madrid.

THE THEATRE
Madrilenians' favourite pastime during this era was the theatre. The works performed in the city's *corrales de comedias* were spectacles that lasted several hours. All kinds of people attended these theatres, from gentlemen and ladies to priests and the humble classes. Men and women were separated, with the latter on the balconies above, called the *gallinero* (hen house) and the former below in the patio.

EL RETIRO PARK

The successor to Philip III was Philip IV, a king more interested in games and entertainment than in the tasks of government. They called him *El Grande* (The Big One), and mockingly said that he was like a hole: the more you take away from it, the bigger it gets. The Spanish Empire was being exhausted by futile wars, and Philip IV did nothing to prevent them. To escape from his cares, the king had the Buen Retiro palace and gardens built. It was like a huge amusement park, where the king and the nobles spent the day having fun, with parties and grandiose spectacles, such as recreations of naval battles in the pond.

LIFE IN MADRID

Accustomed to thinking that it was the centre of the world, the people of Madrid also liked to have fun. Besides the theatre, the streets were full of taverns where they drank and frolicked. Few wanted to work, preferring to spend the day coming up with ways to make some money without making a big effort. They behaved as if nothing were wrong, but the city was dirty, and there were many paupers and beggars in it.

Find the 10 objects that appear in the two illustrations. Some are different colours.

Benigno Vozarrón (Age 8)

If you want to sell something, you have to shout it. You have to blow your horn and yell about how good what you are selling is. Merchants pay you for that. But not just anyone can be a crier. You have to have a good voice.

From 1700 to 1760

Serafín Aguado (Age 6)

In Madrid there are many fountains, but the gentlemen don't like going to drink from them, preferring to have water in cups or jugs brought to them. So, I can earn a little money, to give to my mother at night.

THE WAR OF THE SPANISH SUCCESSION

The last Habsburg king was Charles II, a sickly man who spent his life in Madrid's *alcázar* playing with his dwarves, cared for by doctors and priests. He died in 1700, childless, and his country financially ruined. There then began a war between the French and the Austrians over the Spanish throne. The War of the Spanish Succession was ultimately won by the French, which meant that the new kings would be Bourbons. The first of them to arrive in Madrid was Philip V.

Find the 6 public fountains there were along the Paseo del Prado.

THE BOURBONS

New European Enlightenment ideas and attitudes arrived, characterised by an increasing interest in science and knowledge. In Madrid the Royal Library was founded, along with the first Botanical Garden, along the banks of the Manzanares River, and the Language, Fine Arts and History academies.

Philip V was succeeded by his son Ferdinand VI, who, in addition to putting an end to many wars in which his father had immersed Spain, improved the city with works and laws favouring good relations between residents.

Much of Madrid life then took place on the Paseo del Prado, where the city's ladies and gentlemen could be found wearing the latest European fashions.

Locate these characters in the illustration.

Valladolid   Valladolid   Catalonia   Murcia   Murcia   Andalusia   Galicia   Galicia   Aragón

THE BEST MAYOR: THE KING

Charles III was the third king of the Bourbon Dynasty, and the most popular in the city of Madrid. The *alcázar* of the Habsburgs had been destroyed in a fire, and it was the Bourbons who built a Royal Palace in its place, which still stands today. Charles III, the first king to reside in it, insisted on cleaning, paving, draining and lighting the streets of Madrid. He also created the Watchmen Corps, responsible for lighting and putting out the old streetlamps. He opened more than 30 free schools for girls, set up factories and industries to give the people work, and had the Puerta de Alcalá (arch) and Cibeles (fountain) built, making Madrid more beautiful.

LAS CORRALAS

Many people from other towns and regions of Spain came to the capital looking for work. This was nothing new in Madrid, always accustomed to welcoming newcomers. But the problem of space remained. To solve it they built *corralas*. Arranged around a central courtyard, many people could live in these structures.

40

DISTRICT MAYORS

Madrid's population rose to over 150,000, and to better organise the city it was necessary to appoint mayors for the different districts. Track had to be kept of the people who were constantly arriving to the city, and the new homes that were built. These mayors were also in charge of seeing to urban cleaning, lighting and order, and making sure that there was no cheating with the weights and measures at stores.

FIRES IN THE PLAZA MAYOR

Philip III's Main Square had burned twice, and in 1790 it did so for the third time. Architect Juan de Villanueva, who designed the Museo del Prado (museum), drew up the plans for the new Plaza Mayor, which is that which can be visited today. This was the era of Charles IV, portrayed by the man who was then the kings' court painter: Francisco de Goya. He was commissioned to paint the dome of the chapel of San Antonio de la Florida. Some say that the angels in these paintings are actually portraits of some aristocrats from the era.

Find these scenes in the illustration.

THE BAKERS' DISTRICT
The people of Madrid rebelled several times against the rising price of bread. The Government then decided that all the bakers would live next to the wheat silo, which you can see below, in order to protect them.

Benito Banderilla (Age 7)

The Bourbon kings don't like bullfighting. They say it's a barbaric pastime, and want to ban it. They don't know what they're talking about. It is a festival for the brave, and I'm going to be the best bullfighter in Madrid.

43

Agapito Francés (Age 4)

My mom says that my dad is a French soldier who came to Spain to bring us freedom and democracy, but had to leave because the Spaniards hated him. I don't get it.

From 1808 to 1814

In this illustration there are seven little animals that you will able to find on pages 14-15, 28-29 and 60-61. Find them and you'll able to see, along the way, how Madrid has changed over the years.

THE WAR OF INDEPENDENCE

Through deception and intrigues, Napoleon's army entered Spain, and the royal family was forced to flee to a palace in France. The people of Madrid were the first to rise up against this situation, on May 2, 1808. Looking at the famous paintings by Goya, *The Charge of the Mamelukes* and *The Executions of May 3*, which you can see at the Museo del Prado, you will understand how the War of Independence started. As King of Spain Napoleon appointed his brother Joseph, who came to live in Madrid and tried to win over the people of the city through works improving it. In addition to *Pepe Botella* (Pepe Bottle) and the *Rey Pepino* (*Cucumber King*) the locals dubbed him *the Rey Plazuelas* (King of the Little Squares) due to his habit of placing plazas in the maze of narrow streets that characterised Madrid at that time. During his short reign he had built the plazas of Oriente, Santa Ana, Callao, San Miguel, Santa Clara, Tirso de Molina and others. The French army installed its headquarters in El Retiro park, and after their withdrawal in 1814 the palace and gardens were left in ruins. A year later, King Ferdinand VII entered Madrid.

A CENTURY OF CONFLICTS

The reigns of Ferdinand VII and his daughter, Isabella II, divided the Spaniards with wars and conflicts. Some were supporters of the Constitution, which, adopted in Cádiz in 1812, upheld the equality of all citizens, and condemned abuses by the nobility and the Church. The others only wanted the king to rule, shouting: "Long live the chains!" Many properties of the nobles and the Church fell into the hands of others, and were put to other uses. To all these problems must be added the independence of Spain's territories in the Americas. And Madrid was always the area that most suffered as a result of all these controversies. But good things also happened in the capital, benefitting the people: the gardens of El Retiro park and the Museo del Prado were no longer just for kings, opening their doors to the public. City councillor and chronicler Don Ramón de Mesonero Romanos drafted an Improvement Project for the Capital of Spain, to make Madrid a more modern and liveable city.

Find these characters in the illustration.

Manola Majo Priest Lady Gentleman Barmaid Soldier Singer

Agustina Menesterosa (Age 10)

They keep on changing the name of the Plaza Mayor. Some come along and call it the Plaza de la Constitution, then others decided to call it the Plaza Real, and then they change it again. I don't care because I can't read, but those who can are going to go crazy.

From 1861 to 1900

Mariano Pamplinas
(Age 10)

Early in the morning I go out to distribute newspapers. Then I work in a bakery running errands, and in the afternoon I clean the stables of the carriage company. I want to learn to read, so I can work for the newspaper.

THE INDUSTRIAL REVOLUTION

The end of the 19th century marked a dramatic change in the city of Madrid. These were the years when electricity was invented and, with trains, there appeared the stations of Atocha and Delicias. Many factories were built, and country people migrated to the city to work on them. The population rose to more than 500,000 people, so it was necessary to bring more water from the Sierra de Guadarrama (mountains) through the Canal de Isabel II, the water supply system serving the city. Many houses were demolished to make the streets wider and squares larger. The Puerta del Sol (square) was expanded, becoming the centre of Madrid life. The city swelled beyond its old boundaries, and there appeared new districts, like those of Salamanca, Chamberí and Argüelles.

Count how many horses, donkeys and mules there are in the illustration.

From 1901 to 1935

TERTULIAS AT MADRID'S CAFÉS

Tertulias were social gatherings at cafés like the Pombo, Comercial or Gijón, where intellectuals – writers, artists, politicians and others – got together to talk and debate. Around the tables, people like Valle Inclán, Buñuel and García Lorca chatted about everything from superficial gossip to the political turmoil affecting the country. Many people no longer wanted a monarchy, and preferred another type of government, elected by the people. King Alfonso XIII had to leave Spain, and a Republic was established in Spain.

Eduardo Bandeja (Age 12)

I like to serve the writers' tables. They can really talk. Often I don't understand them, but I don't care. I've never gone to school, but by serving them so much coffee I bet some of their intelligence has rubbed off on me.

Find where these circles are located.

MORE CHANGES

Industrial development continued. The first cars and electric streetcars appeared. The Gran Vía (Main Street) was expanded, and the Ciudad Universitaria (campus area) was built. Everything was changing very quickly, as the modern spirit of progress existed alongside the calm and cheerful life so dear to Madrilenians. However, poor conditions in working class neighbourhoods and factories spurred unions and political parties to demand assistance for those facing the most hardship. They won the elections, but the opposition did not accept this result.

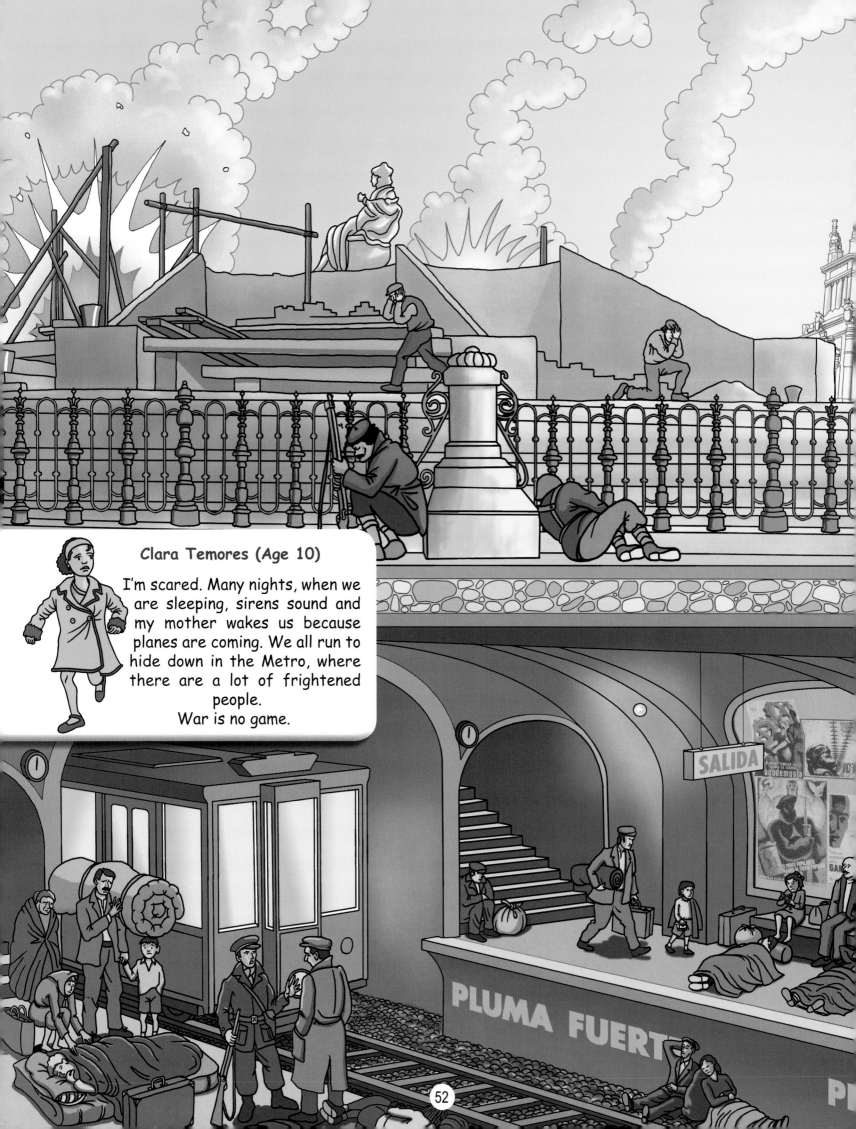

Clara Temores (Age 10)

I'm scared. Many nights, when we are sleeping, sirens sound and my mother wakes us because planes are coming. We all run to hide down in the Metro, where there are a lot of frightened people.
War is no game.

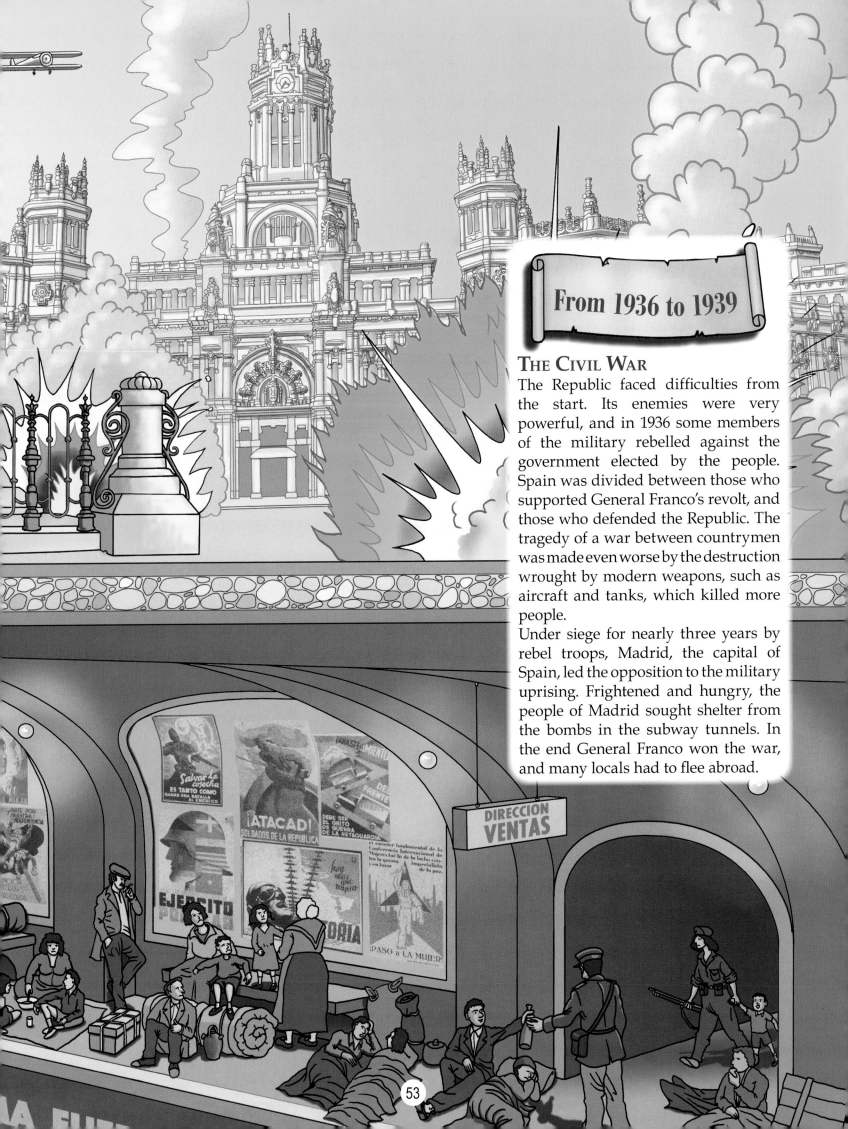

From 1936 to 1939

THE CIVIL WAR

The Republic faced difficulties from the start. Its enemies were very powerful, and in 1936 some members of the military rebelled against the government elected by the people. Spain was divided between those who supported General Franco's revolt, and those who defended the Republic. The tragedy of a war between countrymen was made even worse by the destruction wrought by modern weapons, such as aircraft and tanks, which killed more people.

Under siege for nearly three years by rebel troops, Madrid, the capital of Spain, led the opposition to the military uprising. Frightened and hungry, the people of Madrid sought shelter from the bombs in the subway tunnels. In the end General Franco won the war, and many locals had to flee abroad.

AFTER THE WAR

Madrid soon rose from the ashes and ruins of war. The first years were very tough. Things were lacking, and there long queues just to get something to eat. Gradually living conditions began to improve. Madrid received a flood of people from every corner of Spain. Once again, there wasn't enough space to house all the people. Next to modern residential buildings there were shacks of cardboard and corrugated iron. The newcomers had no other place to go. In the 60s a society of progress and consumption developed. Families could buy cars, and the city grew like never before. In a few years Madrid grew much bigger than it had ever been, up to over 1,000,000 people. More than a dozen towns just outside the city became districts of the capital.

In the illustration there are 7 cats. Find them.

PELUQERIA

Felipito Cuellotieso (Age 4)

My dad is a bank director and makes a lot of money. He bought me a tricycle better than what the other children have. Mom says I shouldn't share it, because the other kids might break it.

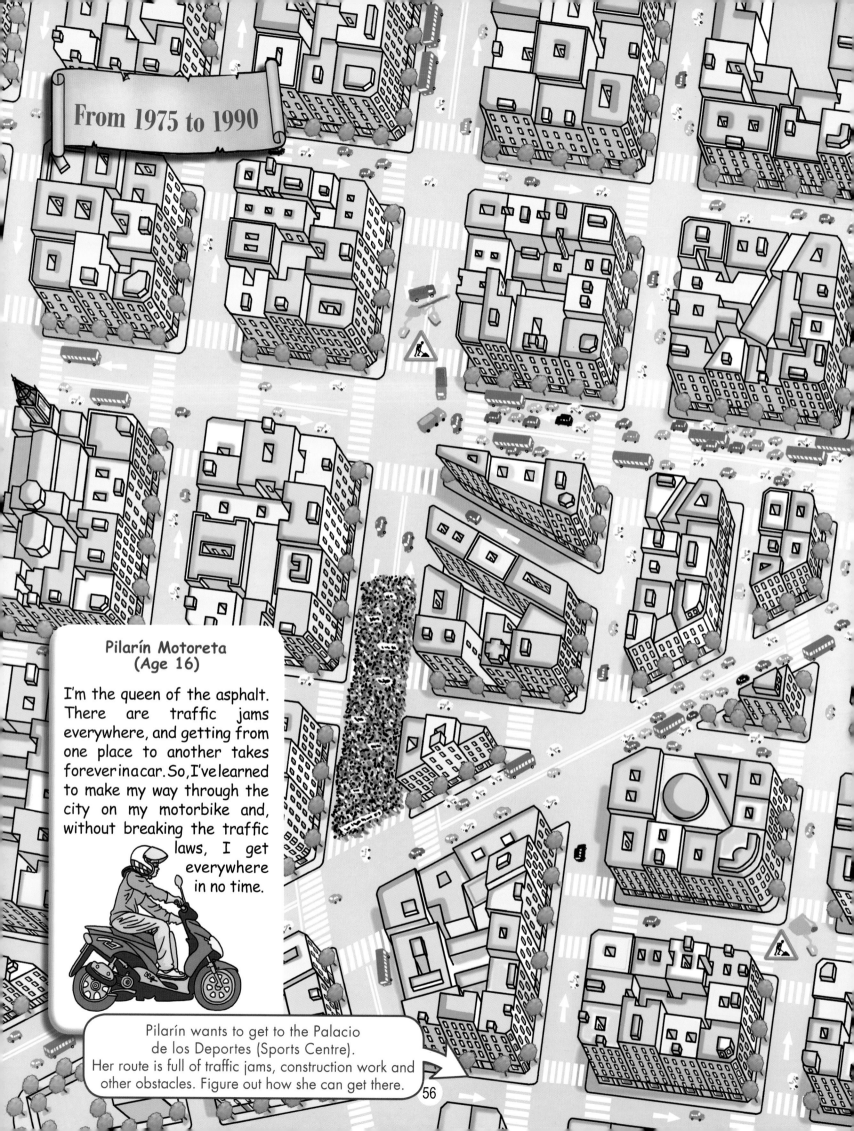

From 1975 to 1990

**Pilarín Motoreta
(Age 16)**

I'm the queen of the asphalt. There are traffic jams everywhere, and getting from one place to another takes forever in a car. So, I've learned to make my way through the city on my motorbike and, without breaking the traffic laws, I get everywhere in no time.

Pilarín wants to get to the Palacio de los Deportes (Sports Centre). Her route is full of traffic jams, construction work and other obstacles. Figure out how she can get there.

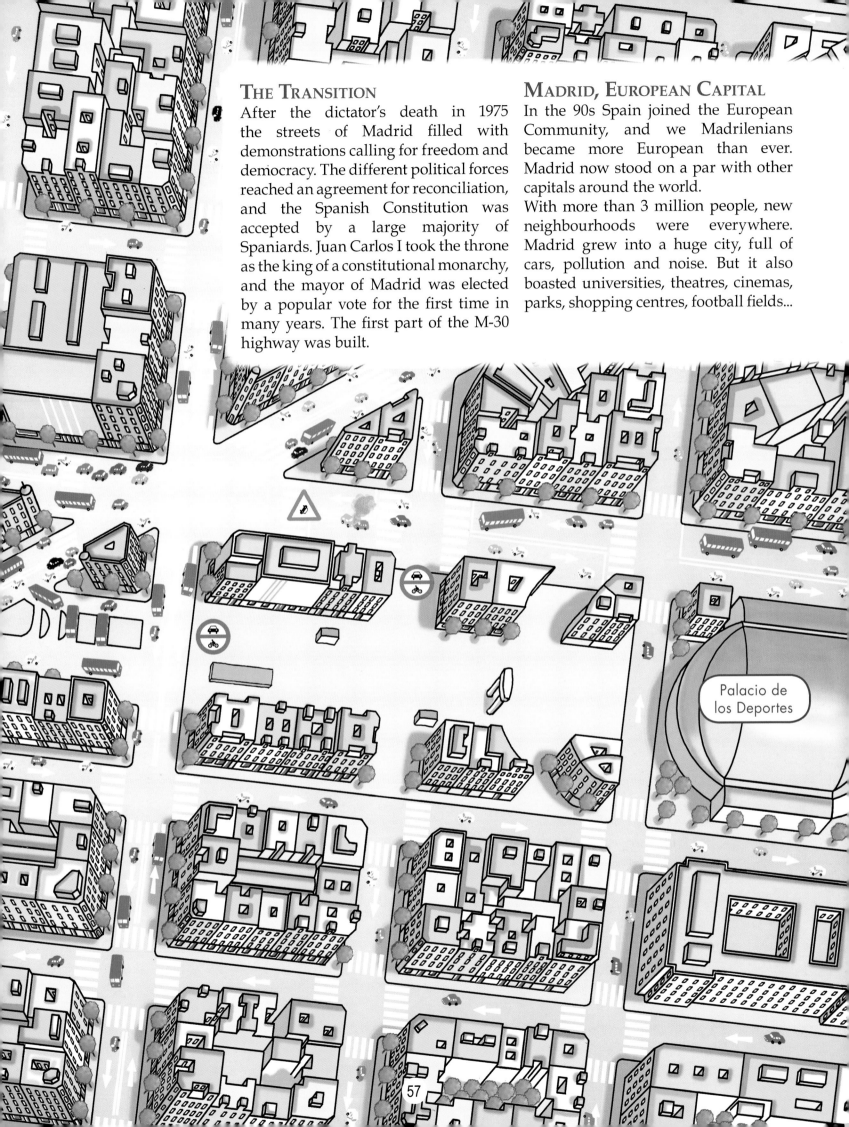

THE TRANSITION

After the dictator's death in 1975 the streets of Madrid filled with demonstrations calling for freedom and democracy. The different political forces reached an agreement for reconciliation, and the Spanish Constitution was accepted by a large majority of Spaniards. Juan Carlos I took the throne as the king of a constitutional monarchy, and the mayor of Madrid was elected by a popular vote for the first time in many years. The first part of the M-30 highway was built.

MADRID, EUROPEAN CAPITAL

In the 90s Spain joined the European Community, and we Madrilenians became more European than ever. Madrid now stood on a par with other capitals around the world.

With more than 3 million people, new neighbourhoods were everywhere. Madrid grew into a huge city, full of cars, pollution and noise. But it also boasted universities, theatres, cinemas, parks, shopping centres, football fields...

Palacio de los Deportes

From 1991 to 2006

MADRILENIANS, CITIZENS OF THE WORLD

The world has changed a lot in recent years thanks to advances in communications. But wealth has not reached everyone. While some countries are rich, others are poor and plagued by war. Remember when many Spaniards came to Madrid looking for work? They did so in search of a better life. Today the same thing is happening. People from the poorest countries in the world come to our city, which, as always, welcomes both newcomers and those born here.

In recent years, new motorways, like the M-40 and M-50, have been built around the city. Next to the new Juan Carlos I Park the Campo de las Naciones convention centre was built, hosting businesspeople and visitors from all over the world.

How many of these characters could be Madrilenians?

José Carlos Djibouti (Age 5)

I want to be a footballer. I'm going to practice a lot, because when I grow up my dream is to play for Real Madrid, the best team in the world.

EL RASTRO

Madrid is a modern city, but still features many monuments, jewels from its past, like the Royal Palace, the Prado Museum and Plaza Mayor, right where they have been for centuries. You can also experience the festive atmosphere of the old street markets by visiting *El Rastro* on a Sunday morning.

In this illustration there are seven little animals that you will able to find on pages 14-15, 28-29 and 44-45. Find them and you'll able to see, along the way, how Madrid has changed.

OVER 1,000 YEARS IN THE MAKING

History never ends because time doesn't stop. Everything is constantly changing, and Madrid is no exception. A city is a living being that, like you, is born and grows. Madrid continues to transform, striving to improve so that its inhabitants can live in peace, harmony and comfort. To understand who we are there's nothing better than knowing where we've came from. If you've read this far, you know a bit more about the origins of your city, the history of its people, and who they are today.

It's time for me to say good-bye, but if you want to see me again all you have to do is look at the crest of Madrid. There I am, next to a strawberry tree, reminding you that there was a time when we bears were also Madrilenians.

61

Solutions to the games (and some comments on each page)

By the colour of the circles you'll know what kind of solution it is, and where it is located.

○ Solutions for each page
○ The seven animals that you'll be able to find on pages 12-13, 26-27 and 42-43 and 58-59.
○ Pages and place where the bear appears.

pages 12-13

Among the most illustrious figures in Madrid's history was the astronomer and mathematician Abu al Qasim Maslama al Mayriti– the last part denoting that he was from Madrid.

pages 4-5

There are 15 mammals from the Quaternary Period and 13 from the Tertiary.

pages 14-15

As nothing has been found to tell us exactly what Madrid was like at that time, we used the oldest images and, of course, our imagination.

pages 6-7

The Roman Road from Zaragoza to Merida passed very close to Madrid. We know that there was a hostel called Miacum, but its ruins have not yet been found.

pages 16-17

There is evidence that Madrid's Council met in the Iglesia de San Salvador (church), which no longer exists. As we were not sure what style it featured, we depicted it as *mozárabe*.

pages 8-9

A 13th-century geographer named Al-Himyari wrote that when the walls of Mayrit were built they found the bones of a monstrous animal, a discovery that caused great astonishment.

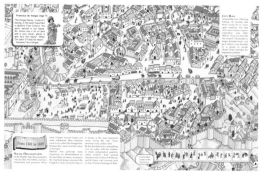

pages 18-19

This image of Madrid in the 14th-15th centuries is imaginary. But to create it we drew upon recent historical studies of what the town was like at that time

pages 10-11

This could have been the old Puerta de la Almudena (gate), later called Santa María. In the background, beyond the wall, you can see the Mozárabe neighbourhood of San Andrés.

pages 20-21

Although it is widely believed that rats spread the plague, the real culprit was mosquitoes.